HAPPY EVER AFTER

A Work Book for Couples Preparing for Marriage

Paul Beasley-Murray

HAPPY EVER AFTER?

A workbook for couples preparing for marriage

© Paul Beasley Murray

Biblical quotations are all from the *Good News Bible* (Bible Societies/HarperCollins)

ISBN 978-1-9999301-1-0

Updated 3rd edition published by The College of Baptist Ministers 2017

CONTENTS

Preface to the third edition

About the author

Acknowledgements

Dedication

Introducing the course

The Course

1. Agreeing the day and the time
2. Getting to know one another
3. Deciding to marry
4. Communicating with one another
5. Dealing with practicalities
6. Discovering the Christian dimension
7. Coming to terms with the past

The wedding service

List of wedding anniversaries

PREFACE TO THE THIRD EDITION

Since the first and second editions were published by the Baptist Union of Great Britain in 1996 and 2003 respectively major social changes have taken place in the lives of those wanting to get married.

In 1996 most people wanting a church wedding were not living together; today co-habitation tends to be the norm. Some believe that moving in together before marriage is a good way to avoid divorce. The logic goes: 'You would only marry someone if he or she agreed to live together with you first, so that you could find out whether you really get along'. In fact research shows that couples who cohabit before marriage (and especially before an engagement or an otherwise clear commitment) tend to be less satisfied with their marriages and more likely to divorce.

Clearly there are couples who have cohabited for many years whose commitment to one another is second to none. As a result there is a tendency, even within the church, to equate such committed relationships with the marriage relationship itself. Yet it is not the same. Marriage involves the making of life-long vows - 'till death do us part'; while co-habitation is a present relationship where the future is ill-defined. Marriage is a public act in which the families as also the community in general is involved (indeed, the law requires that the church doors have to be open during a wedding), while co-habitation tends to be a private relationship between two individuals.

I see co-habiting couples as couples on the way to marriage: although perhaps 'betrothed' to one another, they have yet to fully 'cleave' to one another. Although they enjoy sexual union, they are not truly 'one flesh': sex is an integral part of marriage, but by itself it does not make a marriage. Like most ministers, I am delighted when co-habiting couples wish to commit themselves to one another in marriage, which is a gift of God in creation for family life.

Another change since 1996 has been the increase in the divorce rate as also the increase in the number of children living with single parents. Without making any judgments on the individuals concerned, this breakdown in family life has all kinds of negative consequences for society. There is therefore all the more reason for couples to engage in marriage preparation where the major focus is not so much on the wedding day, but rather on the marriage relationship. At a time when so many things can go wrong, this course wants to help couples discover the difference that Jesus can make to their new life together.

DEDICATION

To Caroline for the way in which she has shaped my understanding of marriage:

'Your love delights me' (Song of Songs 4.10).

ABOUT THE AUTHOR

Paul Beasley Murray is married to Caroline, and together they have four married children and seven grandchildren.

An experienced Baptist minister, he is Chairman of the College of Baptist Ministers. Over the years he has had the joy of preparing many couples for marriage.

Paul is a prolific writer. His weekly blog, *Church Matters* (see paulbeaselymurray.com) includes posts on 'Why not get married in church?'; 'A Christian wedding, not a church wedding' and 'Readings for a wedding'. *Ministry Today UK 1994-2018* contains reflections by Paul on a 'surprise' wedding, wedding photographers, and on 'weddings need not be expensive'; and also ideas for wedding sermons. Ministry Today 1994-2018 is also published by The College of Baptist Ministers – see page 45 for details.

One of Paul's latest books is *Living Out the Call* (Amazon Books, 2nd edition 2016) has been described as 'the most comprehensive practcail introduction to ministry currently avaiable' (Derek Tidball). It is in four volumes: 1. *Living to God's Glory*; 2. *Leading God's Church*; 3. *Reaching God's World*; 4. *Serving God's Church*.

ACKNOWLEDGEMENTS

Almost inevitably with a course that has developed over a number of years, ideas have been taken from various sources. Since it has now become difficult to trace these sources, I wish to make a general acknowledgment of the help received from others who have worked in the field of marriage preparation.

INTRODUCING THE COURSE

Close your heart to every love but mine;
hold no one in your arms but me.
Love is as powerful as death;
passion is as strong as death itself.
It bursts into flame and burns like a raging fire.
Water cannot put it out; no flood can drown it.
(Song of Songs 8.6,7)

A happy and fulfilled marriage is one of the greatest of blessings men and women can ever experience. Yet it cannot be said of every couple that they lived 'happy ever after'. Many marriages do not achieve their God-given potential: some marriages break up, while others become dull and sterile. Hence the importance of marriage preparation. For good marriages don't just happen. Good marriages are the result of people consciously working at their relationship with one another. Your marriage will be successful to the degree that you work at it – both during the period of preparation, as also in the years that lie ahead.

The course assumes that, in addition to the initial interview with your minister, when some of the basic issues relating to the wedding day are sorted out, there will be a number of sessions when you will be helped to think though in a relaxed way what commitment to one another in marriage is all about.

The final section of the book deals with the wedding itself, when you will have an opportunity to finalise the details of the marriage service and to reflect on the meaning of the service.

You will notice that by and large the course is made up of a series of discussion topics, with all sorts of questions to answer. To get the most out of the course you and your partner, before each of the sessions, will need – on your own and together – to work your way through the topics, because some of the questions may require quite a bit of thought before you answer them. Don't be afraid to write in your answers. Nobody is going to grade you on your answers, for - could they do so - there are no right or wrong answers.

It is important too to state that the primary purpose of the course is to encourage communication and discussion, and so facilitate openness between each couple. It is up to each couple to use the material to suit them and their relational needs. The exploring of 'red herrings' may well be as important as adhering to the text.

I hope the course proves rewarding and enjoyable.

1. AGREEING THE DAY AND THE TIME

The Lord God said, 'It is not good for the man to live alone. I will make a suitable companion to help him'
(Genesis 2.18)

It is at the initial interview that the minister will probably decide whether or not he or she is willing to conduct the wedding, and only then can a time and a day be set. There is no uniform policy with regard to weddings – each decision is left to the individual minister concerned. However, no minister will want to marry a couple who just want an excuse for dressing up! Rather the minister will want to ensure that those getting married in church have, at the very least, the intention to take God seriously.

With regard to the marriage of those who have been divorced, guidelines vary from church to church. My policy has been that those wishing to be remarried need to be:

- Willing to recognise that through failing to be faithful to their original marriage vows they have failed both God as also their previous marriage partners. With few exceptions, there is no such thing as an 'innocent' party (as distinct from an 'injured' party). Many ministers feel that a service of re-marriage needs to contain a recognition of such failure and a prayer for God's forgiveness.
- Prepared to learn lessons from the failure of their previous marriage. It is unwise to enter a second marriage without personal growth and development.
- Seeking to come to a place of forgiveness towards their former partners, and not carrying on a continuing vendetta.

- Where applicable, seeking to deal responsibly with the support of their previous partner and, especially, the children of the previous marriage.
- Prepared to take seriously both God and his pattern for living.

At the initial interview your minister will probably want to know the following information:

Your name and address, phone numbers (mobile and landline), and email address

Your future address (if known)

Will the bride adopt her husband's surname?

Your date of birth (and age at the time of the wedding)

Your occupation

Your marital status

If widowed, date of death of partner

If divorced, dates of marriage and grounds for divorce

The names and ages of children (if any)

Your church links (if any)

Your father's full name and occupation (this is needed for the wedding certificate)

Your mother's name and occupation

Will your parents be present?

The proposed date and time of the wedding

The proposed date and time of the wedding rehearsal (often the evening before)

The names of the best man/men and chief bridesmaid/best woman

The names of the two witnesses

The names of any minister/friend and of any musician who you wish to be involved in the wedding

One or two rings?

Special music?

Where will the signing of the register take place?

Flowers? To be arranged by whom?

Printed order of service?

Video recording of the service?

Any other requirements?

Your minister will probably want to mention:

1. Sound/Visual requirements. Most churches insist that any sound/visual requirements are provided at least one week before the wedding. Nothing should be left until the day itself, for otherwise all kinds of difficulties can arise

2. The church's photo policy. Many ministers allow photos to be taken during the service, provided the photographer is not intrusive. It is a legal requirement that photographs may not be taken during the actual signing of the registers, although posed photographs may be taken immediately afterwards. It is important for the couple to decide beforehand on what photographs they wish, and then to give a copy of what they want both to the photographer and to the best man – it is very easy for the photographer to dominate proceedings and to introduce unnecessary delay.

3. Formalities regarding the banns. In the Church of England banns are published at public worship on three Sundays. In other churches, *"Both parties must give a notice of marriage to the Superintendent Registrar of the district(s) where they have resided for the previous 7 whole days. The Superintendent Registrars Certificates may be issued 15 clear days after each notice is given. These preliminaries may take place up to 12 months prior to the marriage."* The 'blue forms' must be handed to the minister at the very latest by the day before the wedding – otherwise the wedding will not take place.

4. Punctuality on the day. While nobody objects to a bride being a minute or so late, it is only right and proper for the members of the wedding party as also their guests to arrive at the church in good time. In particular it is not fair to the

minister and to other church members who have given of their time to help with the wedding for the service not to start on time.

5. Scale of church fees. If the church does not charge a fee, a meaningful donation to the church would be appropriate, as also to the minister and any musicians.

2. GETTING TO KNOW ONE ANOTHER

Your lips cover me with kisses;
Your love is better than wine....
Take me with you, and we'll run away;
Be my king and take me to your room.
We will be happy together,
Drink deep and lose ourselves in love.
How beautiful you are, my love;
How your eyes shine with love!
How handsome you are, my dearest;
How you delight me!
(Song of Songs 1.2,4,15-16)

A – The first meeting

1. Where and when did you first meet one another?

2. What did you like about one another when you first met?

3. What did you dislike about one another?

4. How did you feel about yourselves when you were together?

B – Our present relationship

1. What qualities and strengths have you since observed in each other?

2. What do you appreciate most about one another?

3. In what way do you complement each other and bring balance into your relationship?

4. What interests do you have in common that are a source of mutual enjoyment and pleasure?

5. How does your partner make you feel about yourself when you are together?

6. In what ways do you find your partner difficult to understand? What would you most like to change?

C – Relationships with parents and in-laws

1. How do you feel about your parents and family?

2. How do you feel about your partner's parents and family?

3. In what ways do the two families resemble or differ from one another?

4. What have you enjoyed most in your relationships with them?

5. What problems have you experienced in your relationships with them?

3. DECIDING TO MARRY

Close your heart to every love but mine;
Hold no one in your arms but me.
Love is as powerful as death;
Passion is as strong as death itself.
(Song of Songs 8.6)

A – Making the decision

1. When did you decide to get married?

2. What made you decide to marry? How do you feel about that?

3. (For those living together) How do you think marriage will affect your present relationship?

4. (For those not living together) Going from living on your own to living with another person requires a change in lifestyle. In which of these areas do you think you will need to make changes - time spent with friends? How money is spent? Hours at work? Leisure time? Time spent with family?

5. When you dream about your future, what do you see in three years' time? In ten years' time?

6. Do you hope to have children?

B – Reflections on love

1. When you hear the phrase 'love at first sight', what do you think of? Do you agree or disagree with this expression?

2. Do you believe that 'opposites attract'? If so, why?

3. Define 'commitment'. How do you feel about making a commitment? What, if any, are the conditions?

C – Conditions for a happy marriage

1. What are the most important conditions for a happy marriage? Put the six most important statements in rank order from 1 to 6

    a. The marriage vows are made in church

    b. Neither partner slept with anyone else before marriage

    c. Both partners want children

    d. Both partners have a sense of humour

    e. Making love regularly

    f. Being faithful to one another sexually

    g. Sharing similar beliefs and attitudes

    h. Each partner has other close friends

    i. Each partner trusts the other

    j. Willing to accept change in each other

k. Agreeing on essential needs of housing, clothing and food

l. Agreeing on roles as husband and wife

m. Each partner is able to show forgiveness

n. Each partner is able to give and receive affection

o. Dealing fairly in disagreement and rows

p. Putting the marriage before any other commitment

q. Each partner can communicate feelings and fears

r. ……….. (add your own if you wish) 2

2. How can you help each other to grow and develop?

3. What are your needs for space and togetherness?

4. COMMUNICATING WITH ONE ANOTHER

How beautiful you are, my love!
How your eyes shine with love behind your veil.
Your hair dances like a flock of goats bounding down the hills...
Your teeth are as white as sheep that have just been shorn and washed...
Your lips are like a scarlet ribbon; how lovely they are when you speak.
Your cheeks glow behind your veil.
Your neck is like the tower of David, round and smooth...
Your breasts are like gazelles, twin deer feeding among the lilies...
How beautiful you are my love; how perfect you are!
(Song of Songs 4.1-5, 7)

A – Communicating affection

1. Compare the ways in which your respective parents express affection for each other

2. How does your partner show affection? Do you like it?

3. How do you show affection to your partner? Do you know if your partner likes it?

4. Does either of you use words to show affection? Think of examples.

5. Is there something your partner does to you that you dislike or find unkind?

6. Is there one thing you want to say to your partner today to show your affection?

B – Communicating agreement and disagreement

1. What was the last big decision you made together? Who made the decision?

2. Are you happy with how decisions are made in your relationship, or are there things you would like to see changed?

3. If you couldn't agree on a decision, what would you do?

    - I would decide
    - You would decide
    - We would forget about the whole thing
    - We would ask someone else
    - We would compromise
    - Other

4. How do you each cope with stress?

5. What was your last argument about? Do you think you understood your partner's side? Do you think your partner understood your side?

6. What are the topics that usually start an argument between you?

7. Do you ever fear that your partner will become violent and hurt you?

C – Handling conflict

1. What are the patterns for handling conflict in your respective families?

2. What place does anger have in your relationship?

3. Are you able to resolve your differences or do you bury them?

4. How do you communicate hurt?

5. How do you 'say sorry' to each other? Are you able to sort out things by the end of the day?

5. DEALING WITH PRACTICALITIES

Two are better off than one, because together they can work more effectively. If one of them falls down, the other can help him up. But if someone is alone and falls, it's just too bad because there is no one to help him. If it is cold, two can sleep together and stay warm, but how can you keep warm by yourself? Two people can resist an attack that would defeat one person alone. A rope made of three cords is hard to break.
(Ecclesiastes 4.9-12)

A - Who does what

1. Do you assume that husbands do certain jobs because they are men, and wives have other tasks because they are women?
    - Who will look after the money and pay the bills?
    - Who will clean the house?
    - Who will see to the house repairs?
    - Who will look after the children when they are sick?
    - Who will teach the children discipline?
    - Who will do the food shopping?
    - Who will cook the evening meal?
    - Who will do the washing up?
    - Who will do the washing and ironing?
    - Who will remember birthdays and anniversaries?
    - Who will arrange holidays and leisure activities?

2. Who will keep the fun and affection alive in the marriage?

3. Who will sort out the problems and crises?

4. How different are you from your parents?

B – Handling money

1. Are your family's financial circumstances significantly different from that of your partner's?

2. Is money a source of conflict for you both? What would you like to change?

3. Do you prefer separate or join bank accounts?

4. What effect will having a baby have on your income?

C – Love, sex and children

1. Are your expectations and needs for sex similar or different?

2. Are you able to talk about sex with one another?

3. Here are some words that people use to describe their experience of sex. Underline five words that describe the kind of sex you (would) like?

Exciting	Rude	Embarrassing
Erotic	Warm	Cosy
Boring	Intense	Dirty
Intimate	Loving	Uncomfortable
Mystical	Happy	Pressurised
Animal	Alarming	Energetic
Satisfying	Tiring	Painful
Exploitative	Silly	Annoying
Relaxing	Tense	Angry
Pointless	Thrilling	Sensual
Unifying	Friendly	Ecstatic
Slow	Memorable	Uncontrollable
Passionate	Quick	Threatening
Frightening	Gentle	Compassionate
Sordid	Generous	Urgent
Primitive	Powerful	Emotional

4. Do you think contraception is the woman's responsibility? Have you decided on how long you will wait before you have a baby?

6. DISCOVERING THE CHRISTIAN DIMENSION

A - The Christian difference

There was a wedding in the town of Cana in Galilee. Jesus' mother was there, and Jesus had also been invited to the wedding. When the wine had given out, Jesus' mother said to him, 'They have no wife left'... Jesus' mother then told the servants, 'Do whatever he tells you'. The Jews have rules about ritual washing, and for this purpose six stone water jars were there, each one large enough to hold about one hundred litres. Jesus said to the servants, 'Fill these jars with water'. They filled them to the brim, and he told them, 'Now draw some water out and take it to the man in charge of the feast. They took the water, which now had turned into wine, and he tasted it. He .. called the bridegroom and said to him, 'Everyone else serves the best wine first, and after the guests have had plenty to drink, he serves the ordinary wine. But you have kept the best wine until now'

(John 2.1-10).

1. Why are you getting married in church rather than in a registry office or at some stately home or grand hotel?

2. What place to you want God to have in your marriage?

3. How do you understand Jesus' claim to be the source of "life in all its fulness" (John 10.10)?

4. Is religion a source of conflict for you?

B – God's pattern for marriage

Jesus said: At the time of creation, 'God made them male and female', as the scripture says. 'And for this reason a man will leave his father and mother and unite with his wife, and the two will become one'. So they are no longer two, but one. No human being then must separate what God has joined together (Mark 10.7-9).

1. How independent of your parents are you as a couple?

2. If marriage is for life, then what happens if love begins to fade? To what extent do you agree, "It is not your love that sustains marriage, but from now on, the marriage that sustains your love" (Dietrich Bonhoeffer)?

3. How do you feel about marriage being a commitment for life? If you find yourself at some point attracted to someone else, how will you handle this?

4. If part of God's pattern is to complement one another, in what ways do you complement one another?

C – Love is....

Love is patient and kind; it is not jealous or conceited or proud; love is not ill-mannered or selfish or irritable; love does not keep a record of wrongs; love is not happy with evil, but is happy with the truth. Love never gives up; and its faith, hope and patience never fail. Love is eternal

(1 Corinthians 13.4-8).

1. The Apostle Paul lists eight ways love does not act, and five ways love does act. Try to express in positive terms the eight ways love does act.

2. In the Apostle Paul's original Greek text, there are no adjectives to describe what love is, but rather fifteen different verbs to express what love does. Love for Paul was more than warm cosy feelings. How would you define love?

3. The love described here never grasps, but always gives. What difference does this self-giving love to marriage. How do you feel about love being unconditional?

7. COMING TO TERMS WITH THE PAST

The Lord's unfailing love and mercy still continue, fresh as the morning, as sure as the sunrise
(Lamentations 3.22,23).

A (i) - The past: for those who have been widowed

What are your feelings now about your earlier marriage?

A (ii) – The past: for those who have been divorced or were in a previous relationship?

1. What are your feelings now about your earlier marriage or relationship?

2. How do you feel you failed your previous partner? How did your partner fail you?

3. What lessons have you learnt from the failure of your previous marriage or relationship? Are there areas in which you still struggle?

4. Are you yet able to forgive your former partner for the breakdown of the marriage or relationship? Have you forgiven yourself?

5. What pressures and fears does your impending marriage raise for you?

B (i) - The present: for those widowed

1. In what ways do you think your views on marriage have developed and/or changed as a result of your previous marriage?

2. In what ways is your present partner similar or different from your previous partner? How will this affect your second marriage?

B (ii) – The present: for those who have been divorced or were in a previous relationship

1. In what ways do you think that your views on marriage have developed and/or changed as a result of your previous marriage or relationship?

2. What tensions do you feel you still experience from your previous marriage or relationship?

3. (Where applicable) What arrangements have you made to deal with the support of your previous partner and/or the children?

4. (Where applicable) How often do you see your children?

B (iii) – The present: for those bringing children into the marriage

1. What do the children think of the proposed marriage? How do they view the new partner? How free are they to love openly their absent parent and that parent's parents? Will you find that difficult?

2. What access will the children have to their absent parent?

3. Will everybody be moving into a new home? Have the children been able to share their opinions and ideas?

4. What surname(s) will be used?

5. What will the children call their new step-parent? How do they feel about any step-sibling?

6. How will you handle discipline?

7. What part will the children play in the wedding?

C - The future

1. In what ways are your expectations of your proposed marriage different from the expectations you had of your earlier marriage or relationship? Are there any notable differences?

2. What relationships are still existing (e.g. children) that will affect your proposed marriage? How will you cope with these in the context of a new marriage relationship?

THE WEDDING SERVICE

I pray that your love will keep on growing more and more, together with true knowledge and perfect judgement, so that you will be able to choose what is best. Then... your lives will be filled with the truly good qualities which only Jesus Christ can produce, for the glory and praise of God

(Philippians 1.9-11).

In the final two or three months before the wedding, it will be necessary to discuss with the minister the details of the marriage service. If there is to be a printed order of service, then ensure that you show a draft of the order to your minister before it is printed.

1.   **The Order of Service**

There is no one order of service for a wedding. Some couples, for instance, will want to sing hymns and songs, while other couples may want to have no music at all. It is your day – you shape it as seems best.

The following is one possible order of service:

The entrance of the bride – with her father or another relative; or with her children; or alternatively the bride and groom walk in together

The welcome – given by the minister

Hymn or song

Prayer asking God's blessing on the service

The Marriage

Hymn or song (s)

The Bible readings

The address

Prayers asking God's blessing on bride and groom

Hymn or song

The benediction

Signing of the registers

The wedding procession

2. The Marriage Ceremony

The precise wording of the marriage ceremony may vary. Apart from the legal requirements regarding the declaration of impediments and the consent to take one another as husband

and wife, couples marrying in churches other than Roman Catholic or Anglican may, if they wish to be creative, write their own vows – with, of course, the approval of the minister taking the service. In practice most couples tend to follow the following standard format.

The declaration of the purpose of marriage

We have come together in the presence of God, to witness the marriage of N & N, to ask his blessing on them, and to share in their joy. Our Lord Jesus Christ was himself a guest at a wedding in Cana of Galilee, and through his Spirit he is with us now.

The Scriptures teach us that marriage is a gift of God in creation. It is God's purpose that, as husband and wife give themselves to each other in love throughout their lives, they shall be united in that love as Christ is united with his bride, the Church.

Marriage is given, that husband and wife may comfort and help each other, living faithfully together in need and in plenty, in sorrow and in joy. It is given, that with delight and tenderness they may know each other in love, and, through the joy of their bodily union, may strengthen the union of their hearts and lives. It is given, that they may have children and be blessed in caring for them and bringing them up in accordance with God's will, to his praise and glory.

In marriage husband and wife belong to one another, and they begin a new life together in the community. It is a way of life that all should honour; and it must not be undertaken carelessly, lightly., or selfishly, but reverently, responsibly, and after serious thought.

This is the way of life, created and hallowed by God, that N & N *are now to begin [wish to commit themselves]*. They will each give their consent to the other; they will join hands and exchange solemn vows, and in token of this they will *[each]* give and receive a ring.

Therefore, on this their wedding day, we pray with them, that, strengthened and guided by God, they may fulfil his purpose for the whole of their earthly life together.

The declaration of no impediment

[This legal requirement relates to bigamy or to marrying a close relation]

But first I am required to ask anyone present who knows a reason why these persons may not lawfully marry, to declare it now.

The vows you are about to take are to be made in the name of God, who is judge of all and who knows all the secrets of our hearts: therefore if either of you knows a reason why you may not lawfully marry, you must declare it now

Bridegroom/Bride*: I declare that I know of no legal reason why I ...., may not be joined in marriage to N.*

The question of intent

Will you take *N* to be your wife/husband?

Will you love her/him, comfort her/him,

Honour and protect her/him,

And forsaking all others, be faithful to her/him as long as you both shall live?

Bridegroom/Bride: *I will*

The giving away [optional]

The 'giving away' by the father belongs to a previous era, for today no woman is the 'possession' of any man, and is therefore omitted in most modern wedding liturgies. However, some couples like to retain the 'giving away' as a symbol of the bride's parents' blessing on the marriage:

Who gives the bride away? *I/we do*

A modern alternative is to involve the families or parents of both bride and groom:

Do you, the families/parents of .... and .... give your love and blessing to N & N.? *We do*

Another option is **a congregational promise:**

Will you, the families and friends of N & N, support and uphold them in their marriage now and in the years to come? *We will*

The exchange of vows

I take you to be my wedded wife/husband,
To have and to hold, from this day forward,
For better, for worse, for richer, for poorer,
In sickness and in health

To love and to cherish till death us do part
According to God's holy law, and this is my solemn vow

The giving and receiving of the ring[s]

The rings are symbols of belonging and of unending love

I give you this ring as a sign of our commitment to one another.
All that I am I give to you and all that I have I share with you, within the love of God, Father, Son and Holy Spirit

The declaration of marriage

In the presence of God, and before this congregation, N and N have given their consent and made their marriage vows to each other. They have declared their marriage by the joining of hands and by the giving and receiving of ring[s]. I therefore declare that they are husband and wife. Those whom God has joined together, let no one separate.

The marriage blessing

May the Lord bless you and take care of you;
May the Lord be kind and gracious to you;
May the Lord look on you with favour and give you peace
(Numbers 6.24-26)

At this point the minister normally says: 'You may kiss your bride' – whereupon the members of the congregation often applaud enthusiastically!

A final blessing – normally pronounced at the end of the service

May God the Father give you joy
May God the Son give you grace
May God the Holy Spirit fill your hearts with love
And may the blessing of God Almighty be upon us all.

3. Bible Readings

Favourite readings include:

Psalm 23 (The Lord is my shepherd);

Psalm 121 (The Lord is our protector);

Ecclesiastes 4.9-12 (Two are better than one; a threefold cord is not easily broken);

Song of Songs 2.10-13; 8.6-7 (A song of love);

Matthew 5.1-10 (Happiness is...);

John 2.1-10 (The difference Jesus made at a wedding);

1 Corinthians 13.4-8a (Love is...);

Ephesians 3.14-21 (God's love is all embracing); Ephesians 5.21-33 (The relationship between husband and wife);

Colossians 3.12-17 (God's way of living);

1 John 4.7-12 (God is love)

4. **Traditional hymns**

Favourite hymns include:

As man and woman we were made (to the tune of the Sussex Carol)

For all the love that from our earliest days

Love divine, all loves excelling

Now thank we all our God

Praise my soul, the King of heaven

Often couples like to include modern hymns and songs in the service. It is important to ensure that whatever is chosen is known by a good number of the guests.

5. **Music for the entrance of the bride and the exit of the bridal party**

Traditional music for the entrance of the bride
- Bridal March from 'Lohengrin': Richard Wagner
- Trumpet tune: John Stanley
- Trumpet voluntary: Jeremiah Clarke
- The arrival of the Queen of Sheba: G.F. Handel

Traditional music for the exit of the bridal party
- Wedding march from 'A Midsummer Night's Dream': F. Mendelssohn
- The arrival of the Queen of Sheba: G.F. Handel
- Toccata from Symphony no.5: Charles-Marie Widor

LIST OF WEDDING ANNIVERSARIES

1. Cotton (or paper)
2. Paper (or cotton)
3. Leather
4. Silk (or flowers)
5. Wood
6. Sugar (or iron)
7. Wool (or copper)
8. Bronze
9. Pottery
10. Tin
11. Steel
12. Silk and fine linen
13. Lace
14. Ivory
15. Crystal

20. China

25. Silver

30. Pearl

35. Coral

40. Ruby

45. Sapphire

50. Golden

55. Emerald

60. Diamond

COLLEGE OF BAPTIST MINISTERS

This book is published as an imprint of the College of Baptist Ministers, which is a professional body concerned for the well-being of ministry.

Other books/booklets published by the College of Baptist Ministers include:

A Loved One Dies: help in the first weeks by Paul Beasley-Murray

Ministry FAQs: practical wisdom on areas of church life and ministry by CBM board members

Ministry Today 1994-2018, General Editor Paul Beasley-Murray.

The legacy of 520 articles from the journal Ministry Today UK in 8 volumes, with Introduction, Index and Study Guides.

For further details of these books or to find out more about The College of Baptist Ministers see

www. collegeofbaptistministers.com